Reflections on Retirement in Year One

Happiness Favors a Prepared Mind

Sander Peterson

NEWMAN SPRINGS PUBLISHING
320 Broad Street
Red Bank, NJ 07701

First originally published by Newman Springs Publishing 2023

ISBN 979-8-89061-160-4 (Paperback)
ISBN 979-8-89061-161-1 (Digital)

Printed in the United States of America

To my parents, Harry and Betty Lou. They
were wonderful, supportive, and kind.

To my wife and family, my brother Jon,
my sister, cats, and great friends.

Most importantly, to my Savior, Jesus Christ.

CONTENTS

Preface...vii

Chapter 1: It Begins..1

Chapter 2: Guilt Starts...4

Chapter 3: Guilt Subsides.......................................8

Chapter 4: Sadness...12

Chapter 5: Sadness Accepted..................................15

Chapter 6: Understanding 101 18

Chapter 7: To Be or Not to Be................................22

Chapter 8: A Brighter Time 27

Chapter 9: Redemption 31

Chapter 10: New Beginnings 34

Chapter 11: Keep Climbing......................................38

Chapter 12: The Gold Watch 42

PREFACE

The title of this short book is *Reflections on Retirement in Year One: Happiness Favors a Prepared Mind.* It is a difficult process and not easy to figure out. Maybe, even think of this as a survival guide!

So I'm sixty years old and have worked in accounting for forty years, raising five children through two marriages, currently having eight cats, and leading a fairly healthy life. Last summer, I began to feel sick about managing the extreme responsibilities at work. I was a controller at a downtown organization in Pittsburgh, Pennsylvania, for the past twenty-five years. It was a great job and career, but as a person grows older, things become more worrisome and less rewarding.

There was a time when nothing about work bothered me. Perhaps seventy hours a week was a bit much, but in my case, I was trying to not get fired and learn the job with no orientation or formal training. I had two young daughters and needed to be successful at work. The job was at a prestigious organization, and I was proud to be on the team. It was demanding but special. After many triumphs and challenges, the job began to affect my health, and the downtown commute was a struggle. I began to think about retirement and what that might mean.

I told my boss it was time to retire, and I offered to help train my replacement due to the complexities of the job. There were no notes or manuals to assist in the process, and the newly hired person was unpleasant. It was simply a hands-on approach to cover the basics and allow the new CFO to understand procedures, as well as management of the organization and staff.

After quitting or retiring, I spent the last twelve months going through a process of no work and reflection. It's not as easy as one might think when you retire. It is less stressful, but there are pitfalls regarding how you may feel about your life going forward.

This book contains a mix of personal thoughts and work experiences that might resonate with you. It is a conversation about the five stages of retirement. It seems like a simple transition; but year one requires an honest assessment of what is important to you and perhaps your spouse, family, or friends. It is your new life 2.0.

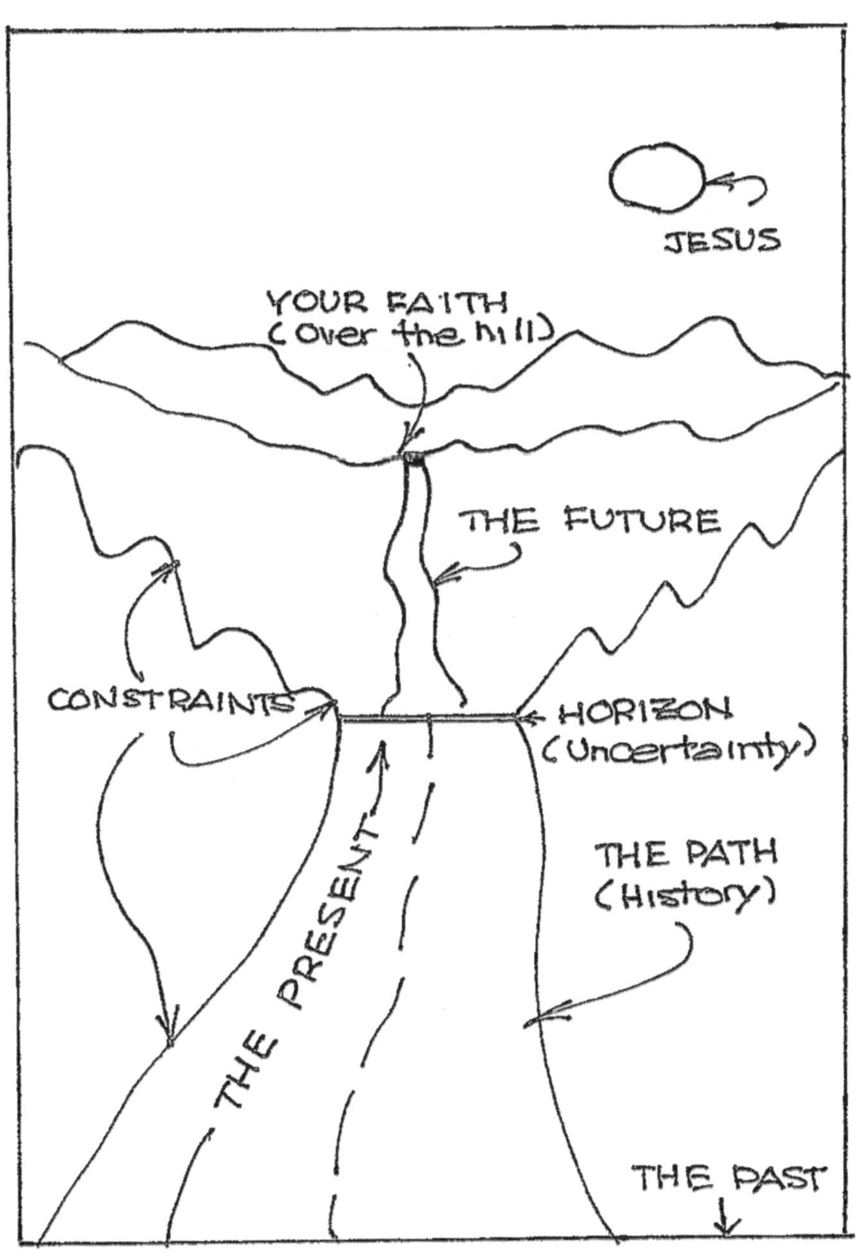

Keith Malinoski

CHAPTER 1

It Begins

I grew up in a small farm town in Illinois, out in the sticks, surrounded by corn fields and a few neighbors. It was a great childhood, with family, love, friends, a swimming pool, and being part of the great American dream—somewhat sheltered from the realities of what others may experience in an urban environment. It was not a bad place to be!

After high school and studying accounting at the University of Illinois, of which I had no idea what accounting even was, it was time to get serious about a career and making money to survive and pay off the student loan. My parents paid for the loan early on, and then Dad said, "This is your problem now." It was fine, and I was blessed to be able to finish the loan payments.

The first ten years were with a retail company as an auditor on the road most of the time. It was a lot of fun to surprise the store managers and staff with a two-week audit and travel throughout the region and start to become self-sufficient as a young person. At the same time, I was naive about how people might feel upon my arrival at their retail store and the possible consequences if there were negative findings to report. However, it was a great experience to learn to write concisely and verbally communicate about important issues. I don't think they cared too much about it as there were more important considerations, such as sales and profit on the docket. In any case, it was very developmental to go through those years.

After moving initially to Pittsburgh, then to New York City, Chicago, Columbus, and then back to Pittsburgh, working for a subsidiary of the retail operation, there was a change coming. I had two young daughters, and the new employer was merged into a huge national firm. It was a bad idea in my opinion. There were layoffs, and many lives were changed. I did not want to move to the new headquarters in Florida even though that seems nice these days despite the hurricanes. A close friend from church helped me to interview at the downtown organization mentioned earlier, and somehow, I managed to get the job and work there for twenty-five years. It's astounding now to realize that I made it through that time without a nervous breakdown!

Okay, enough of my background, but I wanted to set the stage for where things are today. I am now retired and have spent most time working on every project around the house and outdoors in the yard. It has been somewhat excruciating to find meaning in life these days.

At this point, you go from giving orders to maybe taking orders in your troubled mind. Fix this, fix that is the daily routine. Alcohol could be a problem too if you let it. The eight cats are a pleasant distraction, except for the litter boxes!

My wife still works—mostly from home—splits the bills, and pays for health insurance. Thank God! It is a blessing to have support given from her and others with my change in life these days. So after this new routine, I have interviewed at places for part-time employment. The first was at a casino to deal with Blackjack, which could be interesting. The interview was great until they explained it was a swing shift, meaning 8:00 p.m. to 4:00 a.m. That wouldn't work at my age! The group interview was great, and the young woman with green hair seemed to love it. God bless her. There were other interviews until I found a part-time job.

I barely sleep at night and wake up around 4:00 a.m. Of course, each day is the same, and it's hard to remember what day of the week it is. The morning routine is to clean the eight cat food dishes and ready them for my wife to feed the lovely animals around 8:00 a.m. It's okay and gives me something to do straight out of the gate with the darkness outside. I think about how it was to shower, shave, put on a suit and tie, and go to work every weekday, and how glad I am to not have that responsibility anymore. It can be an empty feeling because there is no special purpose on a given day. However, it feels good to not be stressed and on a time line to get to the office for duty.

You used to be the go-to person who knows it all, then you know nothing after retirement and are not as important. It's okay because you are glad to be out of the rat race, constant scrutiny, and measurement as a leader. Thank God that is over. There is some sadness that you are not as important as you used to be at your job, but perhaps, it is good to move on and let someone else carry the burden.

I used to listen to the rock band Bachman–Turner Overdrive (BTO), and the lyrics in one song said, "I love to work at nothing all day." It was great stuff in an alternate universe and reality. They were working on great albums and probably had much, much, more fun than an accountant dealing with the everyday nonsense of operations and management. Oh well, you make choices in life, and that's okay.

So that being said, it's time to explain my thoughts about the past year. There are five stages that have become apparent at this point. They are *guilt, sadness, understanding, pride*, and *new beginnings*.

I think, perhaps, many people go through this process to get to a happy, calm, and responsible place moving forward. Maybe you are one of those retirees, and just maybe this short book will resonate with where you might be in your life. To tell you the truth, I'm not sure where I am yet as it relates to the remainder of my life. But it seems that things sort themselves out, and the future reveals itself each day. I hope so!

The best advice, I think, is to be patient and go easy on yourself until you figure it out. My close friend just retired and promptly had a heart attack the next week. He's okay, but that was a real scare. For you, there is a lot to be proud of over your various jobs, career, family, and at home. So we should try to enjoy the ride and travels into the future. I hope this book, or survival guide, is meaningful for you.

CHAPTER 2

Guilt Starts

Do you remember the feeling of satisfaction with a job well done? Maybe it was a routine task or a major project that challenged your inner being to arrive at a successful outcome. It is an altruistic process in many cases, meaning you work to promote the success of the organization even at risk or cost to yourself. Maybe it even affects your personal life and relationships with others. Oh well, you do what it takes to get the job done.

Sometimes, you wonder about making the right decisions to lead your life into an acceptable place. In my case, that was not an issue as I felt things were moving in the right direction. It's like rooting for your favorite football team for me, the Steelers; and after three consecutive losses and then seven wins, maybe things are in a good place. It's sort of a crap shoot to make decisions that will work for what your future might be. It's hard to say until you go through it and deal with the daily trials and tribulations.

What does retirement mean? One would think it would be a permanent vacation. Maybe it is for a period of time until you feel that you are not contributing to something, whatever that might be. It's fun to golf, play tennis, and go to bars by yourself or with friends. That's great, and it is as those activities have been earned through years of hard labor. But it is not the answer to your future life and meaningful feelings for you or with your spouse and friends. When you retire or quit your job, it is a leap of faith into the future. Who knows what the next twenty or more years will hold if you are lucky enough to have good health? There is a feeling of guilt about not working anymore.

Maybe the word *guilt* is somewhat on the edge of your emotions. The word *guilt* implies that you feel you have done something wrong and need retribution for your actions or desire to retire. I think that we are conditioned over the years to feel that way. We work our whole lives to achieve important results for our company or organization. There is a lot of hard work and conscientious effort to do the right thing and kill ourselves, literally, for our bosses, company, coworkers, friends, family, and acquaintances. Maybe that's okay, but maybe it's an effort to feel you are making a difference. Maybe, just maybe, it is something else.

You grow up as a child, and your parents teach you to achieve some level of success. Through school, mostly high school, you are expected to figure out your interests and possibly your future job opportunities. This isn't easy and, in many cases, is hard to map your course toward college, technical school, a labor job, or some attractive position in the immediate future.

What do you do? I have five children, including two daughters, a stepdaughter, and two step twin boys—great kids and now are young adults. They are all quite impressive and have worked hard through school and college to earn nice degrees. The boys are trying to figure out what they want to do, despite earning finance and physical therapy–related degrees. We discuss the process of starting a career after school and what it might take to succeed. Well, for the boys, that is still in progress; and they are beginning to realize what it takes to succeed and make money and maybe even have future plans to be happy—not sure yet. So it is interesting to think back on those beginning days for me after college.

After working for forty years and feeling pretty good about certain accomplishments, there comes a time when you think about the next stage of your life. You have a nice house, a lovely wife, children, friends, and eight cats. All of a sudden, you begin to wonder why you punish yourself at the office and lengthy commute. There are feelings about working downtown and how cool it is to be a part of that experience. Many people are walking outside and working together in large buildings in a unique and active place. It is fun, and you go out to lunch and see what is happening. Sadly, lots of drugged-up people are lying on the sidewalks as you walk by and go to a nice place for lunch.

What has become of our great country and cities? I guess one might feel lucky to have a college degree and, despite smoking pot in high school and college, make it to a maturity level that is successful and healthy. It is a revelation that you made it this far without a prison indictment. God is good!

So why feel guilty after years of hard work? The missing paycheck is a problem, but there are other reasons why you quit or retire. The looming nervous breakdown is a good one.

Again, why feel guilty? You don't need to, but you feel it is necessary to come to grips with your decision to retire. After twelve months and finding a new part-time job, there is a reflection about what you have done with your life. It feels different to move into a new stage. Possibly, it was a good idea to finally retire. It might be a bad feeling initially, but then you realize you have earned this point in your life to relax a little. It is hard to do and somewhat confounding.

I am sixty years old, and unfortunately, my friends and family members are ceasing to exist or dying to put it directly. It's thoughtful to know wonderful people who are special and are now in a better place. You are taught to believe there is something else after you die, and I believe it! I do. My brother-in-law just passed with cancer. He was a fantastic man that I was proud to be related to. Why do bad things happen to good people? It is an age-old question. He was a superstar and had nothing to feel guilty about. So why do we?

Guilt—it seems like an unfriendly shadow that you don't want to know. We all have it and go through it. After years of hard work and accomplishments, it still exists in the back of your mind. There must be a need to punish ourselves as we go through life. I think that is a good way to have a heart attack. You grow up as a child, a young adult, and then a mature person, and perhaps there is a need to recognize certain accomplishments. It's so easy to be hard on yourself. But once again, you should be proud and thankful for where your life is today. I will explain later about the next stages of your retirement in year one.

When you retire and start a new phase of life, it's truly a new experience. First, you wake up early in the morning and determine what is happening for the day ahead. It is an expected routine to drive to work and perform your job duties with a team around you—nice people that need direction. You finally explain to your assistant that it is time to retire, and there is a lot of consternation about that decision and rightly so. There are people who work with you and depend on your leadership. In my case, I explained that this needed to happen and was probably a good chance for a new person to bring the organization up to the next level. It's a hard pill to swallow.

In any case, it is what it is. There are times in the middle of the night when you might feel the walls are closing in. I have always had a problem with emotions in bed at night. I think that might be normal as you grow older. I don't think it is about guilt but something on your mind that day. I usually get up now at night and try to feel normal again. And then go back to bed and sleep. There are so many commercials at night about natural supplements to help with sleeping. I don't like to take pills and have not gone that route. But you do worry and sweat a lot in bed. I think it's natural. So let's get back to guilt, unfortunately.

Again, when you retire, you feel that you may have given up. My brother said initially that I was a quitter until I explained my mental situation. He gets it now and is very supportive. I mean, I'm sixty years old and burned out at work, I think can be forgiven. Maybe that is where the guilt begins. You've given up at work and maybe at home too. After a while, you begin to understand it is the right thing to do and make the journey back to feeling normal. It seems that patience is the best path and the most healthy one. Don't worry, it gets better!

CHAPTER 3

Guilt Subsides

So I just returned from my brother-in-law's funeral in Utah. Boy, it makes one think about life, health, and family. That man was really special—a great ambassador for what it means to live and give back to people and the community. He passed at the age of seventy-two, on his actual birth date, and will be remembered with great reverence and love. He never retired from work per se but lived life to its fullest extent with my sister. When I was at the funeral, it struck me as a time to reflect on the meaning of being alive and human relationships. We get so caught up in daily responsibilities that it is hard to realize what is truly important.

If you might have a religious leaning, perhaps it's time to think about something else. Maybe we put too much emphasis on our work lives and not enough on the big picture. What is the big picture? Perhaps it is something intangible that has always been there and is a guiding force each day.

Okay, what is the guiding force? Have you ever had a time when your work life is so overwhelming that it is intolerable to continue? That was a daily occurrence in the last year of my professional career. Of course, COVID-19 didn't help the daily mental strain at work and business results, but that is a convenient excuse. Guilt comes into play because you cannot be strong enough to manage the daily stresses of work, meetings, emails, office complications, and the like. As I sit here, one of the eight cats is playing with a ping-pong ball toy. It must be nice, I guess. Simple thoughts are good thoughts and maybe even healthier. Why not be simple and avoid the perplexing thoughts of work that used to exist? The hell with it!

I don't want to get too deep into religion, but there are many gods in the world. They provide meaning, structure, and reasoning about what we are and why we are on the planet. Religion provides a better understanding of each day and a greater appreciation for what we have in our lives, including guilt—that word again. Speaking of guilt, I just left that part-time job previously referred to, which is a first for me. I didn't do anything wrong. A gentle and kind touch on the back of an employee will get you fired these days. What kind of world do we live in? Oh well, life goes on and is an incentive to write this book. It's okay, but what's next? I don't feel guilty about quitting that job by the way.

Back to religion, after retirement, you begin to think more deeply about mortality and the rest of your life—no more daily grind and worries about staff, company, meetings, and profits. Even so, there is a thought about why you are not working in a full-time capacity, as well as concerns about your future life and ability to financially survive.

It is important to plan for the future and make sure that things will work out for you, your family, and your heirs. There is the looming feeling that you are not achieving this goal—in other words, guilt. It's okay. We all have the same issues in some form or fashion. Guilt can be a good thing that might motivate you to work on something or reach out to others that can benefit your life and situation. I always think that you can make a positive out of a negative. In other words, there might be a silver lining that has not yet been recognized. My mother used to say that you need to do things that might be uncomfortable and take a chance. In many cases, that has been true. This makes sense and is not always easy to do. There is, however, a sense of accomplishment when you do take a chance and achieve something new. Why not? You only live once!

All right, so guilt, we have already set the stage for that feeling on previous pages. At the end of the day, I don't really feel too guilty about retiring or, to put it bluntly, quitting the job. It becomes difficult to go to work each day and do the same activities and routine for twenty-five years. Those activities were very meaningful, and I was proud to do that work. It was fun to be in charge of various duties, actually a ton of them. Employees, including management, union, and part-time employees, felt comfortable with true honesty; and together we wanted to create a great work environment. Every job is important and serves a significant role. The night cleaner or labor-intensive positions are just as important as the executives providing oversight.

So maybe the heck with guilt, and you recognize those feelings for what they might mean going forward. Again, no paycheck kind of sucks! You have already decided to forgo that paycheck and rely on your savings or part-time work in the future which is rather unsettling. It begins to wear on you at night in bed. You are not really sure what you are doing and sweat about the future. It's okay. This is normal in my view because times have changed and you need to adapt accordingly. It seems simple, and you get up each day thinking about what to do and what the future might hold long term.

I have been looking for another part-time job to get "out of the house" and make a contribution to feel useful again. Everywhere I go, I ask, "Do you like your job?" and I think if so, what might your business need from a retired person? Everyone is so nice and interested and generally does want to encourage you about possibilities. It's refreshing to know that people are kind at this moment in life.

Perhaps, it's not important to be guilty that you quit your job. Most people don't care as they have enough things to worry about. If you have personally developed a worth about what you did in your job before retirement, maybe it can be more difficult to move on. I don't know. I do know that I have felt pretty good but somewhat empty for the past year and want to try to figure things out. Again, the five stages are *guilt, sadness, understanding, pride,* and *new beginnings.*

All right, let's go with this new thought process and enlightened approach! We are reaching the end of stage one—guilt. It is kind of a dark topic and is important in its own right to acknowledge. So what's next? After guilt, there is a brief period of time to be somewhat sad about your departure from full-time employment. You have gotten through the doldrums of feeling guilty about not working anymore in that relentless fashion, and you need to move on to the next stage—maybe after three months of reflection and working on every possible task at home! That could be good too. However, let's move on.

CHAPTER 4

Sadness

Have you ever experienced a deeply sad feeling about someone or something? It is a feeling that keeps you up at night and gnaws at your inner being. Once again, it is a dark process, but one that we need to go through to get to the other side—happiness! You have worked your entire career to reach retirement with a sense of accomplishment. So you get there and need to feel deeply about the change of life and transition to a new place and time, to boldly go beyond where no one, or you, has gone before—in your own starship, if you like *Star Trek* and science fiction!

Some days are rather good, and some days feel not so good. It goes back and forth from day to day and week to week. It's not all that bad but is somewhat of a roller-coaster ride of emotions. Why do we have to feel this way and not just enjoy the experience of retirement without working anymore? It is human to blow things out of proportion, especially at night for me when thinking about the near and long-term future.

Okay, so why feel sad about not being the person in charge anymore? It's actually not too shabby because the daily pressure of work, meetings, staff management, various issues, or nonsense have all vanished and you don't have to be concerned about keeping the ship afloat. A rudderless ship will get you nowhere fast and maybe even down a hole you cannot quickly dig out of or eventually recover.

You have probably dealt with this overwhelming feeling in your work life. No fun, and it might keep you up at night!

I regret to continue the darkness, but after the *guilt* stage, a new feeling sets in. Hopefully, this is a brief period of time. There is an understanding about the forty or so years you have worked tirelessly at your various jobs, along with managing things at home by yourself, with your spouse or children, including constant property repair issues inside and out. Perhaps you were even involved in time-consuming volunteer or church-related duties. They say that 10 percent of the congregation does 90 percent of the work to keep the church going. I would agree with that concept.

So your life is incredibly busy and rather stressful, but in many ways, it is fulfilling and meaningful. Each day, you drive to work waiting for the next crisis to happen: somebody quits without notice; there is a customer or service-related issue that is screaming at you; or if you're lucky, you can just get caught up with your massive to-do list and a pile of papers on your desk.

Speaking of a pile of papers, my whole desk was covered with project files that would not fit in the four filing cabinets in my office. It was rather embarrassing to have that big mess everywhere, but I did know where everything was located, and it made me look like a busy executive. In any case, I unconsciously wanted to torch the whole thing toward the end when the decision was made to retire. It was a sad feeling to know that the end was near, and whether the knowledge accumulated over twenty-five years could be passed along without feeling concerned the new person would be going up against a tidal wave. I spent months worrying about the problem of leaving the organization in a bind. As it turned out, nobody cared but me.

So the sadness grew into anxiety and concern about the workplace and maybe what kind of legacy might be left in your name and for the new person to carry on. Sometimes you become so caught up in the daily fiasco of responsibilities that you can't look to the future without a sad or desperate feeling about what might be. Again, it is a useless endeavor.

As you read about this second stage, *sadness*, it might be too much to remember how you feel at the time of your pending retirement, or maybe you have things in good shape with the upcoming transition. I hope the latter was true for you, and may God bless your efforts to be ready. Great job! There may have been some lingering projects or problems waiting for further management or your subordinates to deal with, but at least, it is okay to leave.

What if you weren't fully ready to pass the baton and left the next person holding the bag to manage a potential crisis? If you cared, that was me. My fault I guess, but with COVID-19 and the departure of half of the accounting team, it was sadly unavoidable. Looking back at that time, it was ominous to know things forthcoming would be difficult. It was time to retire but not best for your boss, staff, or the organization. Oh well. So you prepare a plan to help the cause at work and try to manage the situation until you leave or when that time is imminent.

So what about this idea that nobody cared about my own retirement transition but me? This seems like a whining opportunity. Oh well, it was nice to know that my career was ending and my team would be stuck with a new boss that was unfamiliar with pretty much everything but was rather sad for the department and sixth floor that we all worked on. My goodness! It was easy after twenty-five years to know the totality of the organization, every department, and the subtleties of the whole job and business. It was not a bad place to be once again, and the daily and monthly duties were very much under control. It took a long time to get there!

And then the pandemic hit in March 2020. Most of the team left because they could either work from home or find a job with greater pay. I didn't blame them and held a small ceremony for each one on their last day, with a staff card, signatures, and something special to remember us. It was nice, but, at the same time, an unsettling event. Well, it was then time to somehow hire a replacement and train the job duties for the new person in addition to everything else. Oh boy. It was not fun, but that's why you are being paid, I guess. It is easy to say but not easy to do. Life goes on and could probably cause you to be somewhat sleepless at night and worrisome. Once again, it bothers you if you care. And I did.

CHAPTER 5

Sadness Accepted

So sadness, what does that mean? I don't know how to explain the feelings you and I may have or maybe will experience. You feel good to retire, but at the same time, you don't know how to begin a life without going to or being in charge of work. It is, once again, a confounding experience. There is an empty feeling that you are not in control of your daily activities or events. It was kind of sad since you worked so hard for this day and years to be retired. We tend to crucify ourselves. Why? Maybe it's just human and normal to criticize or challenge where we are in life. What a joke! We should be proud of the many accomplishments and hard work that was put forth. This will be discussed in stage four, *pride.*

Nevertheless, it is an unkind feeling to be retired and missing out on the previous challenges at your old job. Maybe *old* is a good thing, and we don't know it yet. Perhaps, even being sad about it is likely wrong. We trust that our spouse, friends, and others will understand that it is time to retire. Many people want to work until they are too old to enjoy a healthy and robust life. That's okay because they enjoy what they do. But I was ready to move on and see what happens.

I have a new job now, as a part-time assistant manager at a local retail store about three minutes from where I live. I do like it because there are more responsibilities and it's fun to talk to customers about where they are in their lives. Most of them are retired or starting married lives and new programs with spouses and children. It's interesting to see and learn about where these individuals are headed in their lives. Lots of young children are trying to help Mom or Dad shop, and it reminds me of what it was like to have small children with school and related activities, for sure.

So with my new job, it is enlightening to deal with folks that are buying various items. It is a discount store, and all the prices are around a dollar. The greeting cards are only 50 cents! You can spend at least four dollars per card at other retail or grocery stores. Great cards too! The interesting thing is that because of the recent economy, value-priced stores are growing faster than other popular retailers in our country. Interesting times maybe?

What does that mean? The economy is struggling at the present time. And it's hard to make ends meet for most families. Once again, it is time to evaluate where you are in retirement, maybe in a good place with finances or maybe not. What do you do? Perhaps it might be time to consider a part-time job or another occupation. It is tough to decide after you retired and have not worked much lately, if at all. It is kind of a sad thought too because things have become rather mundane at home without a purpose. There is a great deal of consternation at this point.

For me, the shift from the brutal, full-time finance job to the discount retail store employee is rather stark. You go from sitting at a desk with your trusty computer monitor to standing up and doing tasks that are unfamiliar and physically quite different from the old life. So far, for me, it's a nice change of pace. I have thought about another accounting job based on my skill set but simply can't bear the thought of the nitty-gritty of numbers and the tedious balancing of accounts. Heck, all I really want to do with the numbers these days is balance my checkbook and submit the income taxes each year. That's quite enough after the brain burnout from years of suffering in the exciting world of accounting. I'm being facetious or flippant, I guess, but most employees at the end of the road become somewhat cynical or sad about their relentless jobs. It's a good time to retire!

Now I have to say that things become different at work before you retire when you notify your boss and others that you want to and will retire within the next several months. I agreed to stick around until the new person was hired, and I actually provided training for a period of time to make sure there was a decent transition. Many people have told me that was an admirable thing to do. I thought so too. You want to help the organization at that point because of loyalty and positive feelings built up over time. This approach can backfire because senior management and human resources only care about themselves and don't want a big mess to occur when your twenty-five years of leadership and knowledge disappear. There is a secret dislike that you are leaving, and it might affect the smooth operation that has been relied upon through hard and sacrificial work over the years.

This is a sad situation and probably prevalent for most future retirees that swim the shark-infested waters when changing over to the newly hired person. You are no longer important and are now expendable. Maybe just the sacred two weeks' notice at the appropriate time, on your schedule, is best for you to get the heck out of there! Really, you will most likely never see those people again, so maybe it's best to care about yourself first rather than others in this particular case. If not, you may experience great sadness after maybe being forced out without earned compensation, such as vacation pay. Once the learning period is over for your replacement, things change at work for you. That's what happened to me. Sadly, key people might conspire against you as you leave their rat race behind because they are left with suffering each day and beyond. This is too bad and a bon voyage to those people and their unjust feelings, which is rather sad.

You may carry a sad feeling for several months, along with the guilt already mentioned regarding the unappreciative departure from your years of loyalty to people and the organization. Maybe not, and that's okay too. Perhaps, after a few months, it might be time to get over that feeling of disappointment and bring some closure to the situation. You deserve it, and it's time to find a new purpose for your life and future happiness. Why not? Sometimes you need to dig deep into your psyche, or spirit, to forgive and forget. It's okay because you have sacrificed many things over the years to benefit the organization despite the consequences or buried frustration. I'm sorry this is not too uplifting, but keep reading as things become more resolute, clear, happy, and satisfying over time.

CHAPTER 6

Understanding 101

Hmmm? So we have slogged through the first two stages, *guilt* and *sadness*, which are rather dark and bleak and sort of mind-numbing during the first couple or maybe even six months of your newfound freedom. And maybe it is accompanied by troubled thoughts. Let's not worry too much because I do believe this is normal for a portion of the new retiree populace who actually cared about their jobs and long cherished careers. Now begins the understanding process. It starts, maybe, one day when you get out of bed and realize your life has moved on from the old days of toil to something new and better. Perhaps your breathing is steady and your chest isn't as tight. It sounds good! This may take some time to achieve, so it is important to be patient and kind.

All right, so where are we now? Do we think our emotions are unimportant or maybe less significant because of the short travel through the first days and months of retirement? Once again—*hmmm*—let's think. It's hard to fully gain a new understanding in life because we have been faithful warriors at work for so long. I know this new feeling and try to understand the challenges of a changed life, as well as your life. It's a rather weird feeling because you used to have everything under control. I do get it, and so what?

Who really cares about your relationship with past acquaintances or others you knew at your job or even those that reported to you? They were nice people. It is my experience that you are now a former headline and somewhat forgotten at this point. We need to move on, and that is the beginning of understanding where we truly are at this point in life. It's an epiphany to suddenly realize who you really are as a retired person, and it is worthy of a conversation for us now to discuss! This is our time to take a breath and know that we are at an inflection point.

It was easy to write about and reflect upon the first two stages, *guilt* and *sadness*. There are lots of emotions to drive the conversation between you and me. Now is the tough part to try to understand where we are and where we are headed. For me, I say *hmmm* a lot because for the first time in perhaps forty years, the daily routine at work has ended. Don't be sad because there are new feelings and happy challenges ahead. This is our first class in the school of Understanding 101. These should be fun and interesting days to explore!

I mentioned earlier that we have eight cats, not nine cats and lives! One of them, Milo, was sitting here and would follow me around all day. I wonder what he was thinking when he looked at me, and while I was writing this short book—*hmmm*—it must be nice to be fed and have your litter box changed with regularity and perhaps be thankful for those who take care of you. These are all rescue kittens and cats that were condemned to a tough life and found love, kindness, and redemption in our home. Truly, what are they thinking about these days, and what should we be thinking about as we have been born into a new reality?

Well, that's an interesting question and might be hard to understand. If I were a philosopher, it might be easy to explain and reason the nuances of daily life. But I'm not. Maybe you are not either. Please let me try to discuss this retired situation with some examples.

Exhibit A. After quitting my job, I was obsessed with being busy by fixing every possible repair issue at home. This was great as there were many things to do. In any case, you want to feel that a contribution needs to be made in some form or fashion. Might as well fix and improve the living quarters. Then you can say that you are making a difference and are worthy of being married to your wife. Oh boy, what tangled webs we weave! So after a few months, the projects are done and you are trying to figure out the next steps. *Hmmm.* There are only so many litter boxes to clean each day, probably a good thing as they are no fun to deal with!

Exhibit B. I reached out to old friends from college, as well as a former high school coach, to let them know about my retirement and see what they were doing these days. The high school coach was great and happy to hear from me. He was my cross-country and running coach and was very influential in the early years. Maybe the pain of running five hundred miles each summer was helpful to sustain the relentless effort through forty years of monotonous, accounting work. Who knows? In any case, he sent me a thank-you card with some pictures of our team back in Geneseo, Illinois. Wow, it makes you think about how life has evolved and maybe even thoughts about mortality these days. It was fun to reminisce about that time, and it might be healthy for you to consider reaching out to old friends and mentors. Maybe it might even further your understanding of age and retirement. It did for me.

As mentioned, I called two of my best friends from college. That school would be the Fighting Illini at the University of Illinois. It was great to speak with them and hear their voices from long ago. It seems like only yesterday. Both are still working as a lawyer and a business leader in the Chicago area. I love those guys! To be honest, I felt rather sad or less important that I retired and they were still crushing it in the world. It makes you think that you have given up on being a player in the community. Please don't feel sad. You have contributed mightily to the work life and network of friends and various activities. That is good and plenty to be proud of these days. It is important to realize that and be thankful for your many achievements over the years, as well as to acknowledge the greatness of old friends and family.

It's just an idea that might make sense for you to reconnect with old friends and old times. I believe beginning to understand retirement is also a lonely process. Only you can go through it and start to think about the past, present, and future, and what that really means to you and only you. Your spouse and friends can nurture this process if you want to share your feelings at this point. Maybe that works, or maybe it's best to keep thoughts to yourself alone. These are deep feelings and may take time to fully digest and learn who you are at this point.

That's okay, and we are only human and experience our lives in different ways to allow growth to occur as a person. I have always thought the only way to evolve is to experience adversity. The good times are easy to live each day and celebrate. They are fun, but not much growth is there. It's the hard times, or adversity, that force a person to learn and understand life going forward.

So adversity can be a good thing if the end result is a personal triumph you have achieved and which you perceive as a benefit. This is interesting because your pending or new retirement status has a level of adversity but also a feeling of calmness and perhaps warmth. These are new thoughts as you wake up and spend your immediate time at home without the daily grind of dealing with work problems. Again, this is a time of new thoughts and personal identity to ponder and understand sooner or later. As mentioned earlier, we need to learn at our own pace and be patient and kind. If you are a Type-A personality—in other words, competitive, impatient, and focused on results—then it's time to put on the brakes and relax a bit. Can you do it? I think so if you appreciate where things are now in life, which is not easy.

All right, we have arrived at a place of understanding, rather fully or partially, and that's okay. It's a tightrope to walk the retirement situation and begin to believe that things are okay and maybe a deserved part of our battered but recovering work life. *Hmmm.* I don't like to say that again, but there is much reflection when you have gotten to this point after retirement. Now things have changed in our lives regarding the daily routine, and maybe we have started new activities. That's easy to say and there is hope that our future will be fulfilling and maybe even more special to live out! It's a personal choice and perhaps an easy one. You need to decide.

Let's begin a greater understanding of retirement and where we are as individuals to make choices about life in a brighter way. There is enough of the dark stuff to get to where we are now. At this point, let's think in a positive way together to reach the goal of a happy retirement. Maybe it takes a few months or even a year to achieve. No more negative feelings, please! I think you would agree. Once again, let's move on.

CHAPTER 7

To Be or Not to Be

The third stage, *understanding*, is the toughest part to absorb and, perhaps, comes to grips with as you approach this final semester of acceptance and learning. To be or not to be! So much for Understanding 101, now is the time to run with it and become a person with renewed confidence. Speaking of confidence, did yours diminish? Mine did and didn't need to. It may take time, but you might realize that it's time to think differently. The old life has ended, and the new life and greater understanding have arrived. Thank God! Let's examine this in finer detail with discernment of the current situation, as well as future plans.

What does *discernment* mean? It is the ability to judge well. The day of personal reckoning is upon you and me. How do we judge ourselves at this point in time, and what meaning do we derive to understand things in a greater way? It's time to turn the page and begin to embrace and understand who we might want to be. There are maybe twenty years to go after retirement if you stay healthy and mentally sharp. Maybe you can find new hobbies or make plans to travel with your spouse, friends, or by yourself. These are important considerations so you don't slip away from an active and rewarding lifestyle. Once again, you only live once, so why not take an active role in your own future rather than the old life of toiling for success at work to benefit the organization?

It's time to become your own CEO, or chief executive officer, and guide the path going forward. This could become a daunting task because your own well-being is now involved, along with others at home or in your daily life. As mentioned, early in my career as an auditor, I would travel to business locations and perform reviews to figure out how to improve the operation. Many times upon arrival, it was hard to grasp the totality of that business and identify the most pressing needs. You meet with management to discern the glaring issues, despite pushback from the team at that location. People are busy and too proud to admit certain issues or problems that might exist. Let's face it; we all have opportunities to improve at work, home, or elsewhere. Frankly, there's not enough time in the day to achieve a perfect work environment and compliance with policies and procedures.

One approach to this process might be to scope down or reduce the many issues present and avoid the onslaught of problems to solve. This could also be true as we assess the current situation in or upon retirement. It is a clear and present danger to take on too much when perhaps a measured and less complicated view is better and healthy at this time of transition. Maybe it would be more manageable to take it one day, week, or month at a time and prioritize your activities and feelings as you consider current and future actions. It's time to understand the basics of your newly retired program.

Okay, the basics of your newly retired program. This is worth repeating and reflecting upon. When I think of basics, it means "to establish a foundation to learn and build from"—perhaps with a new starting point in your life, which could be in high school, college, technical school, graduation, starting a new career or marriage, a mid-life crisis, divorce, getting fired, a promotion, retirement, or many other things. The list goes on and on and can even break down to a new month, year, or decade. It's the human condition to deal with changes throughout life, and it can make for interesting and challenging events, as well as times of maturity, crisis, and anxiety. There are lots of prescription drugs or mental therapy that might help, but it is important to think about your past and recent times to make good choices about the future.

You might recall the subtitle of this book is *Happiness Favors a Prepared Mind*. Let's think and prepare together to better understand things at this point. All right. *Hmmm.* Again, it is said that understanding is the beginning of wisdom. This is mentioned in the Bible in Proverbs 9:10. Aristotle was also right that "knowing yourself is the beginning of all wisdom." It seems like a common theme that you and I should think about, understand, and build a solid foundation of greater awareness. I guess, deep thoughts are required here to achieve this goal. And maybe it is a forced process and revelation—*yikes!*—but perhaps a good challenge to consider at our older age and presumed, advanced wisdom, maybe.

Recently, at my new part-time retail job, I was discussing thoughts with a customer about year one of retirement. This resonates with many people. She said, "Well, I believe it is someone to love, something to do, and something to hope for." I wrote it down because it made sense.

She was lovely, and I promised her a copy of this book if it ever gets published. Hope springs eternal!

I have always been a fan of Vincent Van Gogh. In fact, my wife and I visited his and his brother Theo's grave in Auvers-sur-Oise, France, about six years ago. You may know Van Gogh as the painter who cut off part of his ear and was somewhat of a tormented soul despite his brilliance in the late 1800s. He was thirty-seven upon his death in 1890. There is a movie called *At Eternity's Gate* with Willem Dafoe as Van Gogh that struck me from the point of true understanding. He was a painter ahead of his time and died in poverty because his work was not yet understood. In the movie, he stated that sometimes he felt so far away from everything. In retirement, it seems typical to feel that way as things have changed so much from the previous work environment.

In one scene, Van Gogh said to a priest that maybe, just maybe, God made him a painter for people who weren't born yet. Interesting? This struck me as a sublime statement about a reality his tortured mind was beginning to figure out. In other words, it was his personal understanding. He then said to the priest, "Life is for sowing, the harvest is not here. I paint with my qualities and faults." *Hmmm.*

How profound, and what might that mean for us in retirement? We are not perfect, and I do think it's easy to understate one's purpose in life. Maybe, just maybe, we can move on from the past and be thankful for where things are today and what the future holds.

This reminds me of a character, George Baily, in the movie *It's a Wonderful Life*. He was given a chance or fantasy to see what his town, Bedford Falls, would be like if he never lived. His war hero brother would have died as a child in a swimming accident, his loving wife would be a lonely librarian, there would be no children for him to love, and the town would be in shambles due to a ruthless and selfish banker if he wasn't alive to make a difference. It's interesting to acknowledge what each of us contributes over time. It is important to understand our value!

We have worked our whole lives to sow the seeds of a great harvest and perhaps a retired life from the fruits of many efforts. Maybe, just maybe, that is a good thing to realize during this retirement transition. This is something to think about for you and me to better understand. Also, like Van Gogh, we have perhaps made a difference in the future.

So this chapter is entitled "To Be or Not To Be." You probably know that was said by William Shakespeare. Hamlet is in a state of shock and grief as he has discovered that his father was murdered by his uncle. Throughout the soliloquy, at the start of Act 3 and Scene 1, he thinks about whether to face life's hardships head-on or end them by dying. Wow, pretty intense stuff and worthy of reflection as we enter retirement. Please, no suicide for us now, as there is much to enjoy and be thankful for in our past, current, and future life! I pray a lot about family, friends, and good health and selfishly for guidance and forgiveness. That's just me and my faith in God. You may have a different approach, but we might arrive at the same place regarding what our future holds and could mean.

This stage, *understanding*, could be the most important because it helps us to move forward and begin to know what and who we are. The next two stages, *pride* and *new beginnings*, will maybe be easier to read and reflect upon. It seems that after the previous two stages, *guilt* and *sadness*, we might need to forgive ourselves for the feelings of retirement or the "old life" and start to embrace the reality of today.

We ease into retirement with uncertainty about the future and what will become of us. Again, our years of toil and wisdom from work and life experience should be a guiding force to wake up to each day. The ability to understand and acknowledge past achievements and personal growth through success and known failures will move us into a better place. I say embrace this time and be happy now and for the future!

CHAPTER 8

A Brighter Time

The next stage, *pride*, should bring about a brighter and lighter time. More positive thoughts should ensue at this point after the third stage, *understanding*. Let's breathe a little and be thankful for a new and enlightened stage of retirement. It is well deserved! Once again, let's discuss the mantra stated in this book: "Retirement is not a permanent vacation." It is a transition that can easily be dealt with or maybe take time to fully assimilate. The definition of assimilate is to take in information, ideas, or culture and then fully understand. *Hmmm.* It's not easy to do but could be a fun process. I haven't mentioned the word *fun* much in this short book and survival guide, but perhaps it's time to lighten the mood.

So we recently made it through COVID-19, which was a real downer for everyone and even a fatal and very sad situation in many cases. It makes us angry about that curse that devoured our world and daily lives. It was dark and depressing to endure the uncertainty and, in some cases, sickness that caused so much trauma. It is not a bright time for sure but needs to be acknowledged, sadly. Oh well, it was quite terrible. Let's turn the lights on and up despite the pandemic and its effect. Let's move forward with greater awareness of the world around us and perhaps gain a new perspective.

I have tried to write this book in a meaningful way to drill down to the real issues of retirement. To be honest, I'm just a regular person who is trying to deal with the struggles after working forever. It has been a challenge, to put it mildly. At my part-time job, I talk to people like us that have retired or are considering it. It seems, truly, that we all have the same feelings and perhaps some insecurity about the decision to retire. Many customers are very sure in their belief that it was time to quit. I feel that way sometimes, and that's a reason to celebrate. I wish that was me all the time. Most individuals explain their consternation about the change in life. Unfortunately, that's me too and maybe you as well. It is time to be positive.

I am so sick of being sad or disappointed about the end of my work life and the start of retirement. It keeps me up at night and is an inappropriate feeling. Let's let it go! It is easy to say because I feel it most of the time. This short book maybe is therapeutic for us to think about where things are today.

That is enough about my feelings. Where are you in your retirement process? Maybe at the same place as described, or maybe, just maybe, you are ahead of the curve. You may feel strongly about your past, present, and what the future holds, and you should. It is an achievement that needs to be recognized with great pride. Be proud, damn right!

Pride, what does that mean? Is it selfish or narcissistic to feel good about past accomplishments? Maybe it is, but maybe not. Do you remember certain times in your life or career when there was a scary challenge that needed to be met through rigorous and dedicated efforts? Some of those challenges seemed insurmountable at the time because of the expansive effort needed for success. Sometimes the challenge was too much, and you had to either quit or figure out another path to achieve the goal. There's nothing wrong with quitting if the right decision was to reevaluate and move in a different direction. I'm sure that has occurred for most of us. There are other instances where you took on the full challenge—maybe a new product launch, a computer software install, or a new job with more difficult responsibilities, staffing, and reporting requirements. Once again, the list probably goes on and on throughout your work or personal life.

Now that you have retired, or will be soon, it is important to look back and acknowledge what has been done by you and others on your work teams or at home. Retirement is not the end of your journey but rather the beginning. However, one has to think about past success to proudly move into a thankful place and a kind perspective about yourself and the current environment of daily life. This can be a challenge because of feelings of lesser achievement versus previous employment. Pride needs to be fully known by you and only you and must be part of your spirit going forward. Also, if you have chosen to believe in God, there might be strength inside to understand past and current experiences in an intangible way. That is a leap of faith that might be helpful.

So you are retired and have gone through the stages of *guilt*, *sadness*, and *understanding*. Do you sleep better at night, or are things the same? Maybe there is a slight improvement over the past several months. It has been pretty much for me. Well, now is the time the rubber meets the road; or in other words, it is the most important point for something to occur. It is the moment of truth. This sounds ominous but is perhaps a statement of grateful fulfillment for the years of hard work, in other words, retirement!

Anyway, this morning, I went down early to the garage, as usual, to listen to sports or talk radio and plan for the day ahead. When opening the garage door, I saw one of the young kittens, Blackie, sitting on the ping-pong table on top of my outdoor jacket. Sadly, I locked that poor boy in the garage overnight, and he looked disheveled and not used to a night in darkness and despair. He was meowing a lot! I felt bad, of course. He's not permanently scarred but was affected because of being alone all night.

This could be a familiar feeling for a retiree. You are now alone versus the days of constant interaction with staff and customers. Now it's generally known that kittens or cats cannot recollect past experiences to remember and gain strength from the trying times. In fact, they are just lovely animals that live day-to-day without much thought other than lying about the house with an occasional yawn. It's not too bad!

We, on the other hand, as future or current retirees, do think about our past life and experiences to gain perspective about daily issues and the struggle to remain happy and healthy. Again, it is important to look back on previous times or events to meet whatever challenges might occur within a particular day or week. I believe that pride is important to remember how you dealt with both triumphs and adversity, to guide your actions, calm your spirit, and forge ahead with confidence. After all, the definition of *pride* is a feeling of deep pleasure or satisfaction derived from one's own achievements or those with whom the achievement is closely associated. Also, pride is specific to self-esteem, respect, and confidence about who you are and what you have achieved over time.

There are certain levels of pride that can be healthy or destructive. People who are overconfident can become arrogant and more likely to fail. You have heard of the term "pride goeth before a fall." Let's acknowledge that and remain modest about past accomplishments. At the same time, it is acceptable to be proud and confident as you face the future and its daily complications. We need to take on life's responsibilities with a glad heart and kind outlook. I use the word *kind* a lot because it is critical to be kind to ourselves and each other. My wife and I have often felt that most people are too busy with their own lives and don't have time to fully care about others. It seems negative but not really because we all have problems to deal with each day. It is the human condition and an acceptable situation for us to manage issues, as best as possible.

CHAPTER 9

Redemption

The end result of guilt, sadness, understanding, and pride is a greater awareness of where a person stands or belief in oneself. What follows that process is a degree of redemption. It is a complicated word with profound meaning. *Redemption* is defined as gaining or regaining possession of something in exchange for payment or clearing a debt. *Hmmm.* Are we clearing debt or simply arriving at a conclusive moment in our lives? Is redemption part of being proud of past actions or even failures to become the individual we are today? I think so, even in a general sense. In a meritocracy or life, a person is moved into positions of success based on demonstrated abilities over time. This is part of being proud and recognizing past achievements.

As stated earlier, the *pride* stage is supposed to be a brighter time. It can be and should be if we accept the current circumstances at home or a part-time job or maybe some type of repetitive fun event, such as golf, tennis, or a special activity that we like. There are many things for us to do. It is a personal choice to explore and begin a new activity. It could be somewhat daunting. Once again, it might be hard to reach out and develop new places of interest or friends that are not familiar. It seems there are a lot of nice people close by that you could like. I don't know that for sure but think so. It's okay to feel somewhat tentative to make choices to meet others and begin to explore something new.

So we must now move forward with new goals and maybe thoughts of fun and interesting times based on a satisfying feeling of past accomplishments or pride. It is a moment in life to savor and be thankful. At my part-time job, I mention to customers about retirement and what that has meant over the past year. It's interesting because most feel a similar way about the transition and next stage of living. I would say 80 percent of the response has a similar theme of consternation in the early months of retirement. Most people are faced with unfamiliar feelings and the unknowns of daily life. It is somewhat comforting to receive affirmation about my feelings about retirement. And it is ironic to hear how the anticipated greatness of staying home each day can be a challenge for most of us. I think pride is an issue but not for everyone, and that's fine too.

There is a song by the late Eddie Money with lyrics that say "I want to go back and do it all over, but I can't go back I know." Once again, an inflection point to realize there's no going back and mostly a blessing to not have to! Those previous days at work and the many accomplishments were a special time of challenges and achievement. There was probably a lot of stress too. There was much pride to accomplish the projects and various goals that were assigned to us. It might be a good idea to step back in time and think intently about those moments, as well as your efforts to face the tasks at hand. It's easy to forget about the many times each day or week you won.

In retirement, most days become a blur of timelessness and what might be done each day or to even remembering past achievements. *Timelessness* is defined as the quality of not appearing to be affected by the process of time or by changes in fashion. You may feel that way after moving into this next phase of life. To move forward with a feeling of joy and renewed spirit, we must now consider the need to recognize and be proud of the past.

There is a saying that sometimes you have to take one step back to move two steps forward. I believe that is true at this point of transition. It seems logical to use past experiences to gain a better awareness of where our lives are headed. It's a little deep, but it makes sense.

As we remember the past and feel proud about it, maybe it's time to look at our current surroundings and take a moment to recognize where we live and what is happening around us. I get up every morning and think about past struggles and the wonderful feeling of being retired—no more work stress and dealing with multiple employees with multiple problems. It was okay and expected as a manager, but it's nice to have that in the rearview mirror. Let's drive away from those days to get to a more satisfying place and a new destination. We can definitely do it. This is not a time for a midlife crisis. We are at a later stage in life and have moved beyond the proverbial "fork in the road" to now fully enjoy activities of daily life.

We can do whatever we want, within certain parameters, and should take advantage of what is described in the remaining pages of this book—the fifth stage, the *new beginnings*. Please keep reading, and together, we can put the final pieces of the puzzle in place!

CHAPTER 10

New Beginnings

In my kitchen, there are six small signs that are fun to read. From top to bottom, they read, "Coffee pairs nicely with silence"; "All you need is love…and a cat"; "You are about to exceed the limits of my medication"; "A penny for your thoughts, seems a little pricey"; "I drink coffee for your protection"; and "When I die, the cat gets everything." *Hmmm.* They can brighten your day and also be a way to diminish the tightness that exists to relax, have a lighter attitude, and develop a new perspective. I think so and hope you do too! This short book or survival guide has been a journey from the dark feelings of guilt and sadness to understanding, then pride, and now, new beginnings. There is a brighter picture here!

Speaking of pictures, there were four Van Gogh paintings sold in November 2021 at Christie's in New York for a total of 161 million dollars, nearly double the estimates. We discussed earlier that Vincent Van Gogh was an artist who failed to sell works during his lifetime. He was a brilliant and tortured soul who was way ahead of his time and, generally, our time too. That was mentioned in the *understanding* stage and should be acknowledged once more at this point. Not that money is everything but Vincent would be proud of his accomplishments today. This would be applicable as stated in stage four, *pride.* What a superstar he was, and sadly, he wasn't even recognized as a decent painter while living. That's putting it mildly and crazy if you think about it. What a talent and perhaps a blessing for us to appreciate special people from decades or even centuries ago.

As mentioned earlier, my wife and I went on a trip to France and did a river cruise on the Seine from Paris to Normandy. It was quite enlightening to visit Europe and walk on the beaches that were crucial and bloodied when the American and allied forces landed on June 6, 1944. It was very emotional to see the thousands of gravestone crosses and names in perfect alignment at the Normandy American Cemetery. Those men gave their lives for our freedom and saved the way of life that we all enjoy today. There were also women who were critical of the cause. It was a new beginning after World War II and a very costly one, for sure. It was celebrated throughout the world. This is a heavy topic, but as you make decisions to retire and begin to figure out the rest of your life, it is important to appreciate what was done for us in the past! Now it's time for our new beginning after a career of dedicated effort.

Where do we start? What do we do? After all, it is a new beginning. It's probably a good time to shore up your finances and make sure those hard-earned savings are deployed in a manner that will allow for an enriched retirement, as well as provide some leftovers for your family, heirs, or other worthwhile endeavors. When I retired, the first priority was to move or roll over the retirement savings account to a safe investment program. This is the common approach and should be done immediately to ensure the safekeeping of your savings and future income needs. You might want to consider moving your monies or savings right away from your employer and gain personal control over those assets. It might be time to find an investment advisor that you trust to make this happen. Please be conservative in your investments to protect against equity and bond market losses. Get it done!

Secondly, it's time to make sure your estate is properly set up, along with your will and power of attorney. This is critical to ensure your wishes are met regarding your savings and other assets in case your health or situation changes in the immediate future. It's better safe than sorry, or as stated in the Scout Motto, "Be prepared." It's not that hard and doesn't cost much to get this important detail in place. Your investment advisor and associates can do this quite easily with their expertise. Don't be intimidated by the process and make sure the final program is accurate and what you intend at this point. It can always be modified later. This could help your income tax situation as well. Okay, enough of the finances! Let's move on.

It's sort of unsettling because another subtitle to this short book could have been *Nobody Cares*. I don't mean that in a negative way, but the reality is that everyone, even family or friends, has their own issues to worry about each day. Most people, despite good intentions, are concerned about themselves and rightly so. That's okay. Don't be sad or cynical about it. Be glad that certain people have been a significant part of your life and do care about your well-being. It's just that life is so complicated anymore that it is hard to fit other people's problems into the daily equation. That is why I am writing to you to be kind and take care of yourself first during this transition. It is critical. Also, make sure your finances are under control as stated earlier. There is an important truth to saving and spending effectively in retirement. You have reached a point in life to manage your affairs with extreme intention and purpose. End of that topic. What's next?

Well, I'm now retired for a year and need to figure out daily activities in addition to the part-time retail job that has worked out so far. It's fun, and I like it. An older person came into the store yesterday and raised hell because he wanted a refund when the store policy is to provide an even exchange only. It was no big deal, and most customers were fine. He was very unkind and then said he would never come back and I would not be happy when he called my boss to complain. I said that's okay in a disappointed manner. The point is, do we want to be frustrated and sad in life like this unfriendly man, or should we find a way to be happy regardless of the daily stresses in our retirement program? It's always easy to criticize. Maybe, just maybe, we take the higher road and reflect on our blessings and try to be understanding and nice. It's not always easy, but it might help with our blood pressure!

Life is short, and there is a degree of mortality when you reach sixty years old and beyond. There is a song lyric by Jackson Browne that says, "Does it take a death to learn what a life is worth?" It's okay. It is a healthy thought to be getting older. But this needs to be kindly understood as we approach the final chapters of time that we have been given. I hope life has been rewarding for you, your family, and your friends. It should be appreciated every day. You could go golfing, do special or charitable activities, or maybe go out for a meal to make the day more interesting. It's important to find meaning as you ponder personal or pressing issues about yourself, the community, city, nation, or even the world and deal with concerns on a local or macro basis. *Macro* is defined as "understanding the big picture or seeing the forest through the trees." Even though, the trees or specific concerns are important too.

We are headed toward the end of this survival guide and are reaching a jumping-off point now to gather our own personal thoughts and face the upcoming years. They say that this time should be our "golden years." I don't really know what that means, other than a time of greater value and satisfaction. Maybe, I hope so. The final two chapters will hopefully bring about a conclusion and perhaps some inspiration for you and me. As you know, I have referred to the eight cats playing and lying about the house all day. They are rescue cats and are thrilled to be alive and loved. Who really knows what an animal thinks each day? In the simplest terms, they don't fixate on how important they might be. They simply want to be acknowledged. It's just like us when our lives are turned upside down in retirement. Let's try to understand, be proud, and especially, thankful!

CHAPTER 11

Keep Climbing

Upon retirement, it might be tempting to say to ourselves that work life has ended and now is the time to rest, relax, and basically, do nothing. Maybe that is acceptable and fine for a period of time, depending on your personality and need for continued achievement. There's no right or wrong answer to how active the future might be for you. It's a personal choice. The great thing is that it's your choice. There is no boss, board members, staff, or pressing work demands bearing down on you. It's a new freedom that maybe has never been realized. It is your Independence Day, finally!

This is probably a good time to define who you are and make decisions about what is important to you. When you were working, maybe your company, position, and staff limited your scope of thinking. It might be valuable to view retirement as a milestone and an opportunity to think through who you want to be at this point in life. I'm no super pro on retirement yet, but it's just a thought to consider. You will know your own feelings at this point.

Once again, I refer to certain movies that resonate with me in retirement and make a point about where we are in life. It is rather simplistic but could be beneficial to reference right now. If you haven't seen it, there is a movie called *Vertical Limit*. It is about mountain climbers and a brother and sister attempting to reach the summit of K2 in Pakistan. The sister becomes stranded with others close to the top, and the brother, down below, assembles a team of six people to rescue them within twenty-two hours. That was impossible. There is "Montgomery Wick," a mountain man who could help guide the team for the difficult ascent. They need to bring nitroglycerin to blast the small area where the climbers are trapped. At the rescue location, Montgomery Wick says to the brother, "Do you know where you are? You're about 24,000 feet or the Vertical Limit. You can barely stand. It's time to make a choice."

Well, let's make that choice to be strong and serious about life, along with past and future goals. It's okay to gain a new perspective right now, and it doesn't need to be a problem. Another line from the movie is "Strap on the nitro" as they have to carry the dangerous liquid in their backpacks. Presently, I am sitting in my office at home with the cats. It's not too dangerous and, thankfully, no nitroglycerin! But the spirit of this chapter is for us to keep climbing. So let's be true to that endeavor.

Another thought that comes to mind is how you truly feel about yourself versus how others might feel about you. For me, I have always worried too much about living up to the expectations of other people. It's an impossible task and self-inflicted in my opinion. Maybe we should just be proud and confident at this point in life. Who really cares what anyone else thinks? Too much emphasis on the care of other people can be hard on your psyche, confidence, and blood pressure! After retirement and working hard for what seems forever, perhaps it's time to let those worries go away. Of course, it is genuine to conduct your life in a respectable manner. That is what we were taught long ago by our parents. However, without being arrogant, maybe we should just be happy with ourselves and other certain persons and relationships. It makes sense to enjoy who we are in real time.

I'm going to say it again and again, "Be kind to yourself." Please do this and let the past be the past with pride and also great anticipation of a new beginning. What is a beginning? It is an ending in many respects. Things have to end to envision what the future might hold. Endings can be a good thing and a time to wash your hands and embrace the present day. There is a song by the Beach Boys called "Kokomo." My favorite lyric in the song is "We'll get there fast, and then we'll take it slow." Sounds like a good idea, huh? We've been running full tilt for so long at work, at home, in the local area, and way beyond our own backyards. Of course, we have to mow and trim the grass in the yard, which is good exercise for any age. But it's nice to not be in a hurry anymore. Let's take it slow. After all, it is a new beginning!

So climbing is the theme of this chapter. What do we do as we look to the future? That might be sooner or later depending on health and life's circumstances. You may be single, married, widowed, or part of a robust situation with friends and acquaintances. It sounds pretty good if you make the most of where your life is right now and how you want your retirement to be. As stated earlier, it's sort of a jigsaw puzzle to take the pieces of your daily life and put them into a healthy, fun, productive, and enjoyable place where you and others can be happy. It's not easy—maybe—but don't we need to incur ongoing challenges each day, month, and year to have some level of fulfillment? Can we continue to climb to new heights of satisfaction? Of course, we do know this is possible. It's good and should be something to strive for in our destiny. It is a positive choice.

Looking back as a child or young adult, it was easy to see the world and most things in black and white. As we age, it becomes a blur of greyness, and perhaps, there is a yearning to understand what is true or not. It might be wisdom, hopefully, or maybe a greater awareness of the conditions that surround us each day. We might think more about family, friends, or outside influences that could improve the situation or current circumstances.

There are so many things to discern at this point. It can be kind of crazy. And there's more time now to think about it. Topics could be sports, politics, national or global issues, or even basic thoughts about your family, home, or certain relationships. Again, the list goes on and on. In any case, there are choices to be made about the future. These are deep concerns for sure but worthy of kind and positive consideration.

A definitive statement that I find true is "You can't control what you can't control." *Hmmm.* Interesting commentary, in most cases, could be quite necessary to absorb. As we age, it's easy to become a control freak. I don't mean that in a bad way, but it seems we feel our vast experience is enough to know about the intricacy of most issues. Maybe it's true, but I seriously doubt it. However, it's okay to feel that way. There are significant years of hard work and experience to back that up. In reality, we can't control certain issues that are simply not manageable. We can try. That's okay because we do our best to plan for future opportunities and concerns or *new beginnings*. That phrase again!

The last and short chapter ahead is entitled "The Gold Watch." The reason for the name is that many companies, back in the day, would award a gold watch upon retirement for years of dedicated service. That would be very kind for a lifetime of hard work and devout effort. Let's please now finish the journey together.

CHAPTER 12

The Gold Watch

First of all, thank you for reading this book. It has been a labor of love over the past eight months. For real, it has helped me to better understand retirement and come to grips with this new phase of life. I hope for you too.

Once again, the end of work life is not a permanent vacation but rather a time to reflect and understand the efforts to proudly arrive here. As discussed, this is a period of transition that might not be easy or maybe could be a welcome change. Sounds good! I just heard a radio commercial by an investment firm using the term from the *Flintstones* cartoon, "Yabba Dabba Doo!" about the finality and end of the relentless career. This seems appropriate in retirement. It's good and healthy to finally reach that conclusion, but as we know, it's an emotional change from the past and meaningful chapters of your life.

The gold watch, did you get one? I hope so, and that is a proud moment. I did not and basically left the job after twenty-five years with little fanfare. That was fine with me. Honestly, there was no need for special gratitude as it was time to move on and allow a new person to take the reins. As discussed earlier, your value diminishes quickly when you announce retirement. It is what it is but is still a very proud moment.

The good news is that you are finally free to begin the next stage of your wonderful life! What a special time to enjoy with family and friends. There is some consternation about the change in life, but I think this is normal. Besides, it's fun to get up in the morning without a major work problem and deal with homeward issues on each particular day. Let's be thankful for our new place in life! The gold watch was a nice token of appreciation from your employer. But let's not let any piece of metal rust as we ride off into the sunset and beauty of retirement.

To be honest, this is our time and should be appreciated with a clear conscious and glad spirit. We have been blessed with meaningful and cherished careers that have made a proud difference in our lives. What else truly can be asked for? As we move forth, it is important to acknowledge our blessings and "put on the whole armor of God."

Be safe, be healthy, and please enjoy your retirement!

About the Author

Clark Wigginton, Sharpsburg Islands Marina

Sander Peterson lives in Allison Park, which is north of Pittsburgh, Pennsylvania. He is married to Donna Keyser and has two daughters, Rachel and Amanda; and three stepchildren, Barbara, Patrick, and Jonathan. Sander is a certified public accountant (CPA) and grew up in a small farm town in Illinois. He was a controller for twenty-five years at the Duquesne Club, a private organization in downtown Pittsburgh. Together with his wife, they have a loving home, with eight rescued cats, in the North Hills. He is an accomplished pianist and an avid fan of the Pittsburgh Steelers.